Jennifer Capriati

Jennifer Capriati

Ellen Emerson White

SCHOLASTIC INC.
New York Toronto London Auckland Sydney

Photo Credits

cover photos:

© Tom Dipace/Focus on Sports

interior:

1) © Mitchell B. Reibel/Sportschrome East/West
2) © Vandy Stadt/Allsport USA
3) © Simon Bruty/Allsport USA
4) © Loren Hosack/Sportschrome East/West
5) © Scott Halleran/Allsport USA
6) © Tom Dipace/Focus on Sports
7) © Simon Bruty/Allsport USA
8) © Caryn Levy/Allsport USA

ISBN 0-590-44336-4

12 11 10 9 8 7 6 5 4 3 2 1   1 2 3 4 5 6/9

Printed in the U.S.A.   40

First Scholastic printing, August 1991

Jennifer Capriati

Prologue

Every so often, a young tennis player comes along and captures people's imaginations. Chris Evert thrilled the sporting world by making it to the semifinals of the U.S. Open when she was only sixteen years old. Tracy Austin *won* the U.S. Open at sixteen. Steffi Graf, Gabriela Sabatini, Monica Seles, Pam Shriver, Kathy Rinaldi, Andrea Jaeger — the list goes on and on. But none of these athletes stormed onto the tennis scene with quite as much drama and charm as the new ace of the tennis world, Jennifer Capriati.

Jennifer is only fourteen, and she is the youngest player ever to turn professional. Almost every time she sets foot on a tennis court, she sets a new record — the youngest player ever to win a Grand Slam match, the youngest player to win at Wimbledon, the youngest player to win a professional tournament.

Jennifer has been on the cover of major magazines. She has been profiled on television, and HBO even devoted an entire half-hour special to her called "The Building of a Champion." Since becoming a professional tennis player, Jennifer makes headlines everywhere she goes.

Jennifer is the kind of happy-go-lucky player the tennis world has been waiting for. She never stops smiling, even when she is hitting one of her ninety-five miles-per-hour serves. She wins matches, but she also has fun. She may be a professional, but for Jennifer, tennis is a game. After only five months on the tour, she was already ranked number twelve in the world. Her potential as a player seems unlimited.

And, don't forget, she's only fourteen.

Chapter One

Jennifer Capriati was born in New York on March 29, 1976. Considering that she weighed eleven pounds at birth, it was her first dramatic entrance. Soon after that, she and her parents moved to Spain, where they lived until Jennifer was four years old. At three, Jennifer was already playing tennis. When Jennifer's brother Steven was born, the family moved back to the United States, settling in Florida, where they have lived ever since.

Jennifer's father, Stefano, is from Milan, Italy. Mr. Capriati is fifty-four years old, and has done many interesting things in his life, including playing professional soccer in Italy and working as a movie stuntman in movies such as *Patton*. Jennifer's mother, Denise, who is American, is a flight attendant. Her job involves traveling overseas on a regular basis, and she met her husband by a hotel pool back in 1972. They fell in love and were soon married. Although Stefano has now given up his real estate business to manage his daughter's tennis career, Denise is still — at this point — working at her job. But, obviously, she and the rest of the family now spend the bulk of their time on the road with Jennifer and the women's professional tennis tour.

When the Capriatis moved back to the United States, they decided to live in Lauderhill, Florida. Jennifer was only four, but she was already a good tennis player. She spent hours working against a ball machine, never seeming to tire of the game. Her father recognized her natural talent and enthusiasm right away, and wanted to move to a place where Jennifer could develop fully as a player, if that was what she wanted to do.

An American tennis player can, of course, come from any state in the union, but most of the best players are either *from* Florida or California, or move to one of these two states. The main reason for this is that the weather there is so nice and sunny that players can play all year long, and have that much more time to practice and improve. A player from New England, say, is at a disadvantage because of the long winters, and the difficulty and expense of finding indoor courts.

Also, because California's and Florida's perfect

weather makes tennis players flock to these states, the competition is that much better, and a player can advance much more quickly. An ambitious player needs topflight opponents to keep improving his or her game. Families from other parts of the country, who are willing and able to do so, often relocate for the sake of their children's potential careers. Sometimes, this strategy is successful; sometimes, it can backfire by putting too much pressure on the child.

In Jennifer's case, the strategy worked just fine.

A very famous coach lived near the Capriatis' new home, teaching at a place called Holiday Park in Fort Lauderdale. This coach had developed perhaps the most famous player in U.S. tennis history, Chris Evert. His name is Jimmy Evert and, as it happens, he is also Chris Evert's father.

Mr. Capriati brought his little daughter over to see Mr. Evert, and get his opinion about her potential as a player. Well, Jimmy Evert had a rule — he would never teach a player who wasn't at least six years old. Jennifer was so young that he told her father to come back when she was older. But when he saw the way she hit the ball, Mr. Evert realized that this was the best player he had seen since his daughter, Chris. He eagerly agreed to take Jennifer on as a student, and worked with her for the next five years.

As a result, Jennifer first met Chris Evert when she was very young, and they established a friendship that is still very important to both of them today. In fact, on the day of Jennifer's first professional tournament, she stayed at Chris's house, watching television and relaxing. The fact that Jennifer, because of this friendship, was exposed to the highest levels of professional tennis as a tiny child, may be a big reason why she is able to handle the pressures of her high-profile career today. After all, she learned from the very best.

"I really like her," Jennifer said, when asked about Chris Evert at a recent press conference. "I know her as a friend. She was my idol, and I'm honored that people compare me to her."

Mr. Capriati has always been the main coach in her life, but other than that, Mr. Evert has probably had the biggest influence on her tennis game. However, very few players stay with one coach throughout their careers. Different coaches stress different things, and to learn more, a player often has to move on to someone else. Sometimes, this hurts a coach's feelings, but a coach as experienced as Mr. Evert understood how important it was for Jennifer to explore other opinions and philosophies.

Stefano and Denise Capriati knew that their daughter had a chance to become a very fine player, and so, they made another move — this time, to Haines City, Florida. There, Jennifer began to work with Rick Macci, who ran the tennis academy at the Greenlefe Resort. Rick coached

Jennifer for the next two-and-a-half years.

By now, Jennifer was winning junior tournaments, and getting a lot of attention from the tennis world.

Jennifer was on her way.

Chapter Two

Tennis, even at the junior level, is big business. It is also very expensive business. It can easily cost twenty to thirty thousand dollars a year to finance a junior tennis player. There is the cost of equipment — a player runs through a lot of shoes and rackets — plus lessons, tournament fees, transportation, room and board for the many national tournaments across the country, tennis camps, and countless other expenses. Major racket and sportswear companies often give promising juniors some free equipment, which helps. Many top players go to one of the tennis academies, like the Hopman — where Jennifer has spent some time — and Bollettieri programs, which cost thousands of dollars a year. There is some financial aid available, but not enough for everyone.

In many countries — like Germany, for example — the government pays for player development. A player like Steffi Graf or Boris Becker would be selected at a very young age as a possible future star, and the government would take charge of making sure that this child got every chance to play — and would pay all expenses, too. Some people feel that the United States should switch to this system of fully funding athletes, but others feel that this doesn't really fit in with the American spirit of independence and individuality. The bottom line is an American has to pay his or her own way, and tennis is a particularly expensive hobby.

Although there is some help available, in the form of scholarships to tennis academies and corporate sponsorship, realistically, there are only two ways for a family to fund a junior tennis player's career. The easy way is for a family to be very, very rich. But, most people aren't that fortunate. So, the average family in this situation has to make a lot of sacrifices for the sake of the child's potential career. These sacrifices bring some families, like the Capriatis, even closer together, but other families do not survive as successfully.

A junior player deals with plenty of pressure in the day-to-day grind of practice, and the regular tension of tough matches and tournament play. But, when a player also has to think about the fact that his or her family has spent a great deal of money to allow him or her to get this far, the player can feel even more pressure to win, and try to pay his or her parents back. Losing a match means not just letting yourself down, but letting your family down, too. More than one player has had a great deal of difficulty handling this extra financial pressure, but no one has come up with a good solution to the problem.

The United States Tennis Association — USTA — has set up strict rules and guidelines for junior tennis, and the Association regularly revises and tries to improve these rules. In general, junior players are divided into four groups — 12 and under, 14 and under, 16 and under, and 18 and under. National rankings are established in each of these groups, based on matches won and lost in various national and regional tournaments. Regional rankings — for example, New England or the Mid-Atlantic — are calculated, as well as state rankings.

One rule is that while a player cannot, obviously, play in a younger age group, a player *can* play in a tournament for older players. For example, a twelve-year-old can play in the 12 and unders, but he or she can also "play up," and compete in the 14 and unders, the 16 and unders, or whichever group seems most suited to his or her talents.

Since Jennifer was more talented than most junior players could ever hope to be, she rarely played in her own age group. In fact, she regularly won tournaments for 18 and unders.

The three biggest junior tournaments — other than the Grand Slams, which will be discussed later — are probably the U.S. Hard Courts, the U.S. Clay Courts, and the Omega Easter Bowl. In 1988, Jennifer won the 18 and unders in the National Hard Court and Clay Court championships, as well as taking the 16 and unders at the Omega Easter Bowl. It is worth mentioning that she was only twelve years old at the time.

The Easter Bowl tournament was particularly dramatic for Jennifer since she won all of her matches without losing a set. After beating the second seed in the tournament, Erika DeLone, in the semifinals, Jennifer faced the ninth seed, Meredith Gerger, in the finals.

In every tournament, the top sixteen players are "seeded," or ranked, based on their previous match records. This is based on a "draw," or group, of 128 players. In a smaller tournament — with sixty-four or thirty-two players — probably only eight players would be seeded. Then, the seeded players are distributed evenly through the draw, so that the best players don't meet and beat each other in the early rounds. Most fans, even at the junior level, would much rather see players with whom they are familiar, and anyone running a tournament always hopes that the best players don't lose too early, so public interest remains high, right through to the finals. Tennis is, after all, a business, as well as a sport, although at the junior level, the investment is in the future.

Each year, the USTA submits a list of the top junior players to the officials of the Grand Slam tournaments — the Australian Open, the French Open, Wimbledon, and the U.S. Open. These are the top four tournaments in tennis, for both junior and professional players. A victory at a Grand Slam tournament, at any level, will get a player noticed — in all the best ways. A Grand Slam victory will help a player's career the same way an Academy Award helps an actor's career — it is a *very* big deal.

The player list the USTA submits is, for the most part, based on rankings — the United States can only send so many junior players to each of these tournaments, so obviously, they want to send the very best. Sometimes, the player lists cause controversy, since a tournament committee will often select a young junior on the way up, rather than an older junior whose game seems to have leveled off, even if the older player has a better ranking. Junior tennis is *extremely* competitive, and when these player lists come out, players who are left off the lists are always very disappointed, and sometimes resentful. In many ways, junior tennis is even more competitive than professional tennis, since parents are involved in decision-making, as well as players. If Martina Navratilova doesn't get seeded first at a tournament, her mother doesn't call up the tournament committee to complain. Since Martina is in her thirties, it is a good guess that she probably prefers it that way.

Luckily, in Jennifer's case, there was no question but that she was the very best the United States had to offer, and more than deserved to go. She lived up to these expectations too, by getting to the quarterfinals at the 1989 Junior Wimbledon, and winning both the Junior French Open championship and the U.S. Open Junior championship that year. She also won the U.S. Open and Wimbledon Junior doubles championships in 1989. Both *Tennis* magazine and *World Tennis* magazine selected Jennifer as their "Junior Player of the Year" for 1989.

Jennifer had won everything there was for a junior player to win, and she was only thirteen. There is a USTA rule that a player has to be fourteen before he or she can turn professional. There was no competition left for Jennifer in the amateur ranks — but she was only thirteen. As soon as her birthday came, it would be time to turn pro. All she could really do now was wait.

Chapter Three

Jennifer may be one of the best tennis players around, but she is a completely normal teenager who likes Tom Cruise, Johnny Depp, and going to the mall. She likes going to the mall *a lot*. She likes the Simpsons, and Sweetarts, and reading Danielle Steele novels. She likes M.C. Hammer and Paula Abdul and eating Twizzlers.

"I like music," Jennifer said recently. "I like to go to the movies, I like hanging out with my friends. I just went to the Prince concert. I didn't like him before, but now I really love him."

While waiting around to turn fourteen, Jennifer moved again. This time she and her family moved to Wesley Chapel, Florida. Jennifer would now go to school at the Palmer Academy, while working on her tennis at the Harry Hopman program, affiliated with the Saddlebrook Resort. She had a new coach, former touring pro Tom Gullickson, and she dove into her new program with enthusiasm.

At Saddlebrook, players are kept very busy. On an average day, Jennifer would practice tennis in the morning, then go to school for five-and-a-half hours, then return to the courts for three more hours of practice. She would also work in an hour of Nautilus. Her days rarely ended before seven-thirty or eight o'clock in the evening, but she was making lots of progress. She was becoming a better player than ever.

What type of player is Jennifer Capriati? Of course everyone knows that she is a very *good* player, but what sort of style does she use? What are the strengths and weaknesses of her game? Where does she most need to improve? How good can she become?

"Basically, I'm a baseline player," Jennifer says, "but I'm trying to become an all-around player. I like to return serve."

There are three basic types of tennis players. One is the baseliner. The baseliner is, predictably enough, a player who spends most of her time back at the baseline. A baseliner, typically, has excellent ground strokes — backhand and forehand — and can keep rallies going forever. She is a very steady player, but not always aggressive, waiting for her opponent to make a mistake instead. A good base-liner makes very few unforced errors, and wears down her opponent by sheer consistency. Steady, patient, and slow are adjectives often applied to this style of play. This is why baseliners are so successful on the slower surface of clay courts, like at the French Open. Chris Evert is the most famous example of this type of player, and many young players have adopted her style, right down to her two-handed backhand, in the hopes of duplicating Chris's success. Of course, there is only one Chris Evert, and while her ground strokes were phenomenal, her true strengths were her unrivaled mental toughness and competitiveness. Although coaches try to teach that mental attitude, the truth is, it cannot really be learned — you have it or you don't.

The second type of player is the serve-and-volleyer. This is, again, a self-explanatory term. A serve-and-volley player is a player who relies on an overpowering serve, and excellent ability at the net, to win. It is a very aggressive style of play, and not nearly as common as it used to be. This type of player is often taller than average, since height adds speed to a serve, and allows for better court coverage up at the net. This sort of player tends to have the most success on grass courts, like at Wimbledon. Pam Shriver is an example of a classic serve-and-volleyer.

The final type of player is probably the ideal type — the all-court (or "all-around") player. This is a player who does *everything* well. Although some might describe Martina Navratilova as a serve-and-volleyer, she is probably more accurately described as an all-court player, because there really aren't any weaknesses in her game. An all-court player needs both natural athleticism *and* the determination and desire to practice long hard hours to fully develop her game. Often, a naturally talented player will not work as hard because she has never *needed* to work as hard. Hana Mandlikova — who may have been the most talented player ever to play on the women's tour — was a very good example of this. If Hana had had anything *close* to Chris Evert's tenacity and power of concentration, she would have broken every record in the book. But, what makes sports interesting is the human factor — there is no such thing as the perfect player. A perfect player would be more like a robot. Everyone — even a Martina or a Steffi Graf — has some kind of weakness. It can be as simple as getting a terrible headache or a sprained ankle during a match, or as big as an ineffective serve or poor ground strokes.

Younger players tend to be baseliners. This is because a smaller player can win without much trouble from the baseline, and because it is easier to develop ground strokes than it is to learn a big, booming serve. A player needs to grow into a serve-and-volley game, both literally and otherwise. A serve-and-volley game matures as a player matures. But, with today's high-tech rackets, a young player can stand back at the baseline and hit the ball as hard as anyone else. Not only are rackets much bigger than they used to be — it is rare to see a player with a traditionally sized racket; most of them use either the midsize or the oversize versions — these rackets are also made out of materials like graphite and Kevlar, which add tremendous power to the frame. Until the last ten or twenty years, all players used the same small wooden rackets, and precision and finesse were important facets of a player's game. Today, with the new super-rackets, a less technically accomplished player can succeed because the racket will compensate for mistakes and miss-hits. The same principle exists in baseball — as baseball gloves have gotten bigger, players catch more balls than they did in the early days. As tennis rackets have gotten bigger, tennis players miss fewer balls — it's as simple as that. But, a player can get only so far with a good racket — after a while, weaknesses begin to catch up, and the holes in a player's game become very obvious.

After all that, what sort of player is Jennifer Capriati? Well, her analysis is correct — right now, she is a baseliner on her way to becoming an all-courter. On the one hand, her ground strokes are terrific, and she has a two-handed backhand; on the other hand, her play is fast and aggressive, and her serve is as fast as a Roger Clemens fastball. As Jennifer grows taller, and practices even more, her serve should get better and better.

Because Jennifer has spent so much time with

Chris Evert, and was coached for five years by Chris's father Jimmy, people assume that her game is identical to Chris's game. Actually, except for the two-handed backhand, there aren't many similarities. Jennifer makes many more mistakes, but she also makes shots Chris would be unlikely even to have attempted. Jennifer is less steady, but much more daring.

Jennifer has powerful, accurate ground strokes, but she is developing a strong net game, too. She is not afraid to come to the net, and will often drive back a short shot from her opponent, following her momentum to the net to put the return away. Jennifer's first serve is excellent — and will only get better as she grows. Right now, she is almost 5′ 7″, and could be 5′ 9″, or even taller, when she stops growing. Her second serve still could be better, but even in the short time that she has been playing professionally, her improvement has been dramatic. Since a second serve is not hit as hard as a first serve — to avoid double-faulting — it is important to hit the second serve deep into the opposing service box, and often, with some sort of tricky spin on the ball. Jennifer is learning this.

Jennifer is very fast, but more important, she has excellent instincts on the court. The fastest player in the world won't be successful, if she doesn't know *where* to run. Zina Garrison is a good example of this. Zina is, perhaps, the quickest player on the tour, but it has taken her a number of years to develop the court sense that makes her such a fine player today. This is the sort of concentration and understanding of the game that Hana Mandlikova was never really able to develop. A player needs to anticipate where her opponent's ball is going, and be there, ready to hit it before it gets there. No one ever thought of Chris Evert as being fast, because her anticipation was so good. Jennifer has the same sort of natural instincts, both in her ability to be in the right place, and also, in her ability to place the ball where her opponent *isn't*. This last skill may be even more valuable.

A player with decent court sense knows to hit the ball into the open court, with the idea that it will be harder for her opponent to get to it. A player with *brilliant* court sense anticipates the direction in which her opponent is going to go, and then, hits the ball *behind* her. It is much easier to get to a ball when you are already heading in that direction; it is almost *impossible* to reverse direction in time to get *back* to a ball. Jennifer has uncanny court sense for a thirty-four-year-old player, forget a fourteen-year-old. This ability will win her many matches that she would otherwise find difficult.

People have many different opinions concerning the specifics of Jennifer's tennis game, but it would appear that she has a few very special gifts, above and beyond mere physical talent. These gifts concern the mental part of her game. A smart athlete will always last longer and achieve more than a merely talented athlete. A Martina Navratilova, who is both, is as rare as a Magic Johnson, who is also both. Jennifer has the potential to join the stratosphere where this sort of athlete exists.

One of Jennifer's great gifts is that she just plain "goes for it." This is not as easy, or as common, as it sounds. Often, a player will give up when she is way behind, or play conservatively when she holds a lead. The best way to lose a match is to play *not* to lose. And, once again, this is an ability that cannot be taught. A player is born with it.

Coaches are often full of clichés about not changing a winning game, and going with what got you there in the first place. Like most clichés, these ideas have a basis in fact. If you start changing your game to suit your opponent, or the score, or the weather, or whatever the case may be, you will not play your best. If you have a powerful first serve and are winning your match, but then start worrying that you might double-fault, odds are, you *will* double-fault. If you hit the ball hard, keep hitting the ball hard. If your strength is spin serves, and you suddenly start trying to blast aces — it isn't going to work. A coach's advice would be to stay with your strength, and work on your weaknesses in practice. The coach would be right.

This is one of the things that Jennifer does better than anything else. She goes for her shots. Watching Jennifer play, it would be hard to guess the score. She is an attacking player, so she attacks. When she is ahead, she keeps attacking. When she is behind, she attacks some more. This attitude will help her pull out of a lot of tough matches as her career goes along. Maybe it's just as simple as not trying to be something you're not. Jennifer plays to, and with, her strengths, and that's smart.

Jennifer is also an intense competitor. Since she is always smiling off the court, many people make the mistake of assuming that she is also laid-back *on* the court. She is as tough and focused as a player can be. On the court, she is all business, rarely losing her concentration. Considering the amount of media attraction she has gotten — before, during, and after matches — this is nothing short of amazing. But, Jennifer is a player who never loses her cool. This is good for her, and this is good for tennis as a whole. There have been too many players in recent years who waste time throwing tantrums.

What are Jennifer's weaknesses as a player? In general, her game is very solid, but even the best players in the world can always work on *something*. Jennifer's serve, particularly her second serve, needs some improvement — but, not much. She also makes a lot of unforced errors. One reason for this is because she plays such an aggressive, slashing sort of game, but as she goes along, she will have to cut down on the number of errors. Most coaches believe that you can always teach a player to control her shots, but that it is much harder to teach a player to hit with force and power. So, this part of Jennifer's game will naturally improve — and except against the top three or four players in the world — it hasn't exactly hurt her so far.

There are those who feel that Jennifer plays too quickly. She is so swift and energetic that these observers feel that she rushes *too* much, and must learn to vary her tempo a little. Mainly, this means that she should slow down *between* points, as opposed to *during* points. Sometimes, it is a good idea to take your time, give your opponent time to think about things and get nervous. But, Jennifer is so eager and enthusiastic that she rarely even pauses to take a breath. Again, as she gets older, she will develop these nuances.

After all — in case you haven't heard yet — she's only fourteen.

Chapter Four

The United States Tennis Association and the Women's Tennis Association decided to let Jennifer turn pro right before her fourteenth birthday, in time to play in the Virginia Slims tournament in Florida, where she lives. Virginia Slims sponsors most of the tournaments on the women's tour.

The tournament was held in Boca Raton, Florida, and Jennifer made her debut on March 6, 1990, about three weeks before her fourteenth birthday. This made her the youngest professional player in the history of the game.

For most players, turning pro is almost an anticlimax. Amateurs are allowed to play in professional tournaments, but they are not allowed to accept prize money. So, when a player signs in at a tournament, she must check one of two little boxes on her entry form — either the one that says "Pro" or the one that says "Amateur." And, once that little "Pro" box is checked, a player is a professional, even if she never wins another match again. If she doesn't win, she isn't likely to be on the tour very long, since she won't be ranked high enough to get into tournaments, or make enough money to support herself, but turning pro is surprisingly easy. And once you become a pro, there is no turning back. Bo Jackson, who plays both professional football and baseball, found this out the hard way. When he went to get his team physical to play pro football, this made him ineligible to play amateur *baseball* anymore. A tennis player who turns pro cuts off the option of ever, for example, playing college tennis. So, it is not a decision to be made lightly.

But, Jennifer and her family, and coaches, had given all of this a great deal of thought, and they knew they were doing the right thing. So, Jennifer was now a professional tennis player, without having played a match.

Almost all professional players have agents to handle their business affairs. Agents are there to give advice and help guide a player's career, particularly when it comes to deciding on a schedule of tournaments to play, and deciding which company endorsements to accept. There is so much money in the game today that an agent is really a necessity. An agent will handle all of a player's financial affairs, and let her just concentrate on playing tennis.

Jennifer's agent is John Evert, who is with the International Management Group. IMG, along with firms like ProServ and Advantage International, is an agency that specializes in handling tennis players. John is, as it happens, Chris Evert's little brother. The Evert family has been more than a little influential when it comes to Jennifer's tennis career.

John Evert was very busy right from the beginning as companies got in line, hoping that Jennifer would endorse their products. Naturally, companies that manufacture tennis equipment want tennis players to endorse their particular products, but other companies, looking for just the right image, also seek endorsements from athletes. If an athlete drinks a certain thirst-quenching drink, or wears one special watch, this endorsement can influence sales.

Not wanting Jennifer to take on unnecessary responsibilities, John Evert has been conservative in accepting offers. Jennifer has signed two major contracts, although others are certain to follow. Diadora, an Italian sportswear company, has signed Jennifer to an estimated five-year, three-million-dollar contract. There are incentive clauses in the contract, as is true for most athletes, and if Jennifer wins a certain number of tournaments, or reaches certain high rankings, she will

be paid more. In return, she wears Diadora clothes and sneakers when she plays. In fact, as far as Diadora is concerned, the more often she wears Diadora fashions, especially when she is in the public eye, the better.

Diadora gives Jennifer all the tennis clothes and shoes she needs, whenever she needs them. All she has to do is wear them.

Jennifer's racket contract is with Prince, and it is a three-year contract, estimated to be worth at least a million dollars. There are also, of course, incentive clauses built into that contract. In return, Jennifer uses Prince rackets exclusively. This is good business for a racket company, since fans often buy the same kind of racket their favorite player uses. Jennifer Capriati is a lot of people's favorite player.

Most tennis players today make more money from their endorsements than they do from actually playing and winning tournaments. This keeps a lot of agents very, very busy.

It has been reported that Jennifer spent the day of her first professional match in Chris Evert's nearby home, hanging out with her parents and her brother Steven, watching television. Chris was away at the time, since her being there might have added even more pressure to an already big day. The tournament was being held at Boca Raton's The Polo Club, and there were thousands of fans and reporters waiting to see tennis's newest phenom. Reporters had come from all over the world, and every one of them wanted an interview. Exclusive, if possible.

Jennifer's first round opponent was Mary Lou Daniels. Mary Lou, ranked 110th in the world, had been a pro for ten years. Jennifer hadn't even been pro for ten minutes. As Jennifer and Mary Lou walked onto the court, there were so many photographers waiting that the match had to be delayed.

"I was a little overwhelmed," Jennifer has admitted since, when asked how she felt about facing that many members of the press. "It was so crazy. But, it's calmed down, and I think I'm getting used to it."

Jennifer may have been a *little* nervous after having had to wait so long for the court to be cleared and play to begin. After starting off with a quick 3–0 lead in the first set, suddenly Mary Lou came back and was winning, 6 games to 5. But then, Jennifer won the next game, forcing a tiebreaker, which she won easily, 7–1.

In tennis, depending on the tournament rules, players either play regular sets or tiebreak sets. In a regular set, a player has to win by two games. So, while six games usually win a set, if the score were 6–5, a player would have to win another game to win 7–5. Sometimes, it can take a long time for a player to get two games ahead, so tiebreak sets were introduced to make matches shorter, and they are used in most tournaments now. In a tiebreaker, players play to win the best of twelve points — in other words, seven points. But, again, a player has to win by two points, so if the score is 6–6, the player would have to win the next two points to win 8–6 — a two-point margin. This can take a while in a close tiebreaker, but it takes much less time to win two extra *points* than it does to win two extra games. Tiebreakers are only used at the end of sets, and the winner of the tiebreaker is declared the winner of the set. Since Jennifer won seven of the first eight points, she and Mary Lou didn't even have to play the full twelve points in their tiebreaker.

The easy tiebreaker must have done a lot for Jennifer's confidence, because she breezed through the second set, 6–1, to take her first professional match. Afterwards, Mary Lou gave her the supreme compliment of comparing Jennifer to Steffi Graf, the number one player in the world. Clearly, Jennifer belonged on the professional tennis tour.

Jennifer's second round match was against a German player, Claudia Porwik, who was then ranked 34th in the world. Jennifer's play was uneven, as she won the first set, 7–5, then got wiped out, 6–0, in the second set. But then, Jennifer came back to win the third set, and the match, to move on in the tournament.

Jennifer had a tough match in the third round, facing a French player named Nathalie Tauziat, who just happened to be the 16th-ranked player in the world. Jennifer got behind early, 4–1, and it looked as though she would probably lose the match. But Jennifer, with her attacking style of play, is the sort of player who can come from behind, and that is what she did. Before Nathalie really knew what was happening, Jennifer had won the next five games in a row to take the first set, and then steamrolled her way through the second set, 6–2, to win the match.

In the fourth round, she was up against Helena Sukova, ranked number 10 in the world. Helena, at 6' 2", is one of the tallest players in the game. She is from Czechoslovakia, and has a strong serve-and-volley game. Helena was not a player a thirteen-year-old brand-new pro should be able to beat. But, Jennifer slammed through the first set, winning by a 6–1 score. Helena was winning 4–3 in the second set, when it began to rain, and the match was delayed for half an hour. When play resumed, Jennifer won the next three games in a row, and the match was over.

So, in her very first tournament, Jennifer was in the semifinals, a truly remarkable achievement. Her opponent was Laura Gildemeister, number 21 in the world. Both of the sets that they played went to tiebreakers, and Jennifer won both of them. And now, she was in the finals. The young star was living up to all of the advance publicity and more.

"In my first pro tournament, I really didn't expect to get to the finals," Jennifer said. "It's great, but it was a surprise."

The other finalist was Gabriela Sabatini, the

number three player in the world, who was to win the U.S. Open a few months later. Gabriela, along with Monica Seles and Steffi Graf, is one of the greatest young stars in the game today. Now, Jennifer was hoping to join this exclusive group of players who are the future of women's tennis.

Jennifer played a tough match, but Gabriela's skills and experience were just too much, and Jennifer lost, 6–4, 7–5. After the match, Gabriela told the press that she had had to play her very best tennis to win. Jennifer might not be one of the very top players in the world — yet — but nobody doubted that she soon would be.

Jennifer also played doubles in the tournament, partnered with former tennis great, Billie Jean King. Although they lost in the second round, the combination of the bright new star and the brilliant legend was fun for everyone to see.

Jennifer's debut was even better than anyone might have dreamed. As a new professional, Jennifer had won nothing but respect and admiration. The fans and the media alike were both eager to see what she would do next.

Chapter Five

Jennifer's next tournament was the Lipton International Players' Championship, held in Key Biscayne, Florida. She lost in the fourth round — also known as the round of sixteen, which was a more than respectable showing.

By now, Jennifer had appeared on the Women's Tennis Association computer with her first world ranking, and she debuted at number 25. This was the highest computer debut of any player in history. Jennifer set yet another record.

After that happy news, and now officially fourteen years old, Jennifer moved on to the *Family Circle* Magazine Cup at Hilton Head, South Carolina. Amazingly, Jennifer made it to the finals again, in only her third tournament, defeating two highly ranked players on the way. She beat top-ten player, Arantxa Sanchez Vicario, another one of the new young stars in women's tennis. Arantxa, still in her teens, already has a Grand Slam championship — the 1989 French Open — under her belt. Jennifer's victory over her was impressive, indeed.

Then, in the semifinals, Jennifer played against nineteen-year-old Natalia Zvereva, seeded sixth in the tournament and currently ranked in the top-fifteen in the world. Unlike baseball, where the World Series involves only teams from the United States and Canada, in professional tennis, players really *are* from all over the world, and a top-ten-in-the-world ranking really does mean that you are one of the best ten players in the world. Natalia is from the Soviet Union, while Sanchez Vicario is from Spain. Very few countries are *not* represented on the professional tennis tour, it would seem.

Jennifer won her semifinal match easily, beating Natalia by a score of 6–0, 6–4. The entire match took less than an hour. Natalia did her best to fight back in the second set, trying to slow down the tempo of the match with looping ground strokes from the baseline, but Jennifer countered that by coming to the net and put the match away.

In the other semifinal, a Czechoslovakian player named Regina Rejchrtova lost — and a player named Martina Navratilova won. Jennifer would be facing her biggest challenge so far as a professional. It was only her third tournament, and she would be playing her sixteenth professional match. Martina, on the other hand, was going for her one hundred and fiftieth career singles championship, and had played over thirteen hundred professional matches. In fact, she was playing professional tennis three years before Jennifer was even *born*. Before the match, Jennifer cheerfully told the press that she was excited that she would be playing "a lege," which means "legend" in Capriati speak.

Jennifer's match against Martina showed how very far she had come as a player — and how far she still had to go, to be one of the very top players in the world. Jennifer played hard, and she played her game — and Martina played better.

The match was on national television and, for the first time, the whole country had a chance to get a good look at Jennifer. It is unlikely that anyone turned the television off, disappointed by this glimpse of the future.

The final score was 6–2, 6–4, but Jennifer played with fire and enthusiasm throughout, hitting 26 shots for outright winners. Martina was better, and faster, but Jennifer made the match closer than anyone would have expected. Even though she was never really ahead, Jennifer kept taking chances and going for the tough shot, displaying for the national television audience a game of impressive maturity and depth. The "lege" just displayed a little more maturity and depth.

Match point was typical of the kind of player,

and person, Jennifer is. Martina hit a booming serve, then came in to the net, hitting a beautiful forehand volley that was called out. But, Jennifer shook her head and came up to the net to tell the umpire that the ball *had* been in. The umpire decided to overrule the "out" call, and because of Jennifer's good sportsmanship, the match was over and Martina had won the one hundred and fiftieth singles title of her career. And Jennifer had won even more fans than she already had. Very few players would make a call against themselves at matchpoint in a tournament championship.

"I wasn't even expecting myself to go out there and win," Jennifer said, "but I knew it would be a learning experience, and a fun one."

Jennifer was well on her way to becoming a "lege" herself.

Chapter Six

After Hilton Head, Jennifer's next stop was Europe, and the Italian Open. Since Jennifer's father is from Milan, it was fun for her to be playing in Italy. Many players use the Italian Open as a warm-up tournament before the French Open, one of the four Grand Slam tournaments, which takes place shortly after the Italian Open.

Being in Italy was exciting, and many of Jennifer's Italian relatives came to see her play. Jennifer was able to take time to do plenty of visiting and sightseeing in Rome — and her fair share of shopping, too.

In the tournament, she made it to the quarterfinals. Along the way, Jennifer had beaten a crowd favorite, an Italian player named Laura Golarsa. It took three sets, with the fans clearly rooting for

Laura, but Jennifer finally won, and earned her own cheers. She also earned a chance to play Gabriela Sabatini again. Gabriela had beaten her back in Florida, at her first professional tournament. Jennifer did her best, but Gabriela was able to beat her again, in two straight sets, 6–2, 7–5, and move on to the semifinals.

The Italian Open is a tournament Jennifer would particularly like to win someday, in front of all her relatives, and in the next few years, there's a good chance that she will.

How, exactly, does the women's professional tennis tour work? Professional women's tennis has really only been around since 1970, when a group of "renegade" players, led by Billie Jean King and Rosie Casals, broke away from the standard, non-paying women's tennis tour to form a professional tour of their own. The going was slow, but with the emergence of young Chris Evert a year later, and the slow accumulation of corporate sponsors, the women's tennis tour began to become a realistic way to make a living.

In 1973, the Women's Tennis Association was formed to oversee the tour, and the WTA still runs women's tennis today. The WTA's board of directors consists of twelve touring pros, several of whom are always among the top players in the game. This board meets regularly to discuss, among other things, new corporate sponsors, how players' computer rankings should be determined, how many tournaments a very young pro should be allowed to play, and other issues affecting the tour. The USTA and the Women's International Professional Tennis Council also get involved with some of these decisions.

In fact, up until Jennifer came along, the rules governing a young pro's first year on the tour were very rigid. A player who had yet to turn fifteen was only allowed to play in twelve tournaments a year, and only ten of these tournaments were allowed to be major events, like Grand Slam tournaments and Virginia Slims events. The idea behind this rule was to allow young players to adjust to the tour gradually, so they wouldn't get burned-out.

But, the WTA and the Women's International Professional Tennis Council had not dealt with a player like Jennifer before. Jennifer has risen so swiftly, and confidently, through the ranks of women's tennis that it is hard to force her to comply with normal standards. There is an exception to every rule — and, obviously, Jennifer is it. Now, the rule has been amended so that professionals under the age of fifteen are allowed to compete in twelve tournaments — which can be major or minor — and, in addition, they are allowed to enter the Virginia Slims Series Championships at the end of the year, if they qualify. Only the top sixteen players in the world are allowed to enter the prestigious Virginia Slims Series Championships. Jennifer had a good chance to qualify.

Most people have heard of the Virginia Slims

tournaments, but there is more to the women's professional tour than that. The next rung down is a series of tournaments called the "Ginny" circuit. These tournaments are best suited for players with rankings below forty or fifty in the world. They are not as important as regular Virginia Slims tournaments, nor do they offer nearly as much prize money, but they are easier to get into — and because many top players skip them — easier for a lower-ranked player to win.

Below the Ginny Circuit is the lowest rung of professional tennis, known as the USTA Satellite Circuit. These tournaments are good for players ranked below one hundred and twenty, say, and they are even better for amateur players trying to build a ranking. Good showings in satellite tournaments may result in invitations to Ginny tournaments, or even Virginia Slims events.

Results from all three rungs of the women's tour are counted in the computer rankings. A Virginia Slims victory is worth more points than a Ginny victory, which is worth more points than a satellite tour victory. A player can win a satellite tournament, and not get as many points as a player who loses in the second round of a Virginia Slims tournament. For example, if a player ranked 60th beats a player ranked 40th, that victory does not get as many points as a victory over a player ranked 20th in the world. One of the reasons Jennifer debuted on the computer at 25th in the world was that at her first tournament — a Virginia Slims tournament — she beat players ranked 10th and 29th in the world.

Jennifer was, without question, a brilliant player, who would have very little trouble getting invited to tournaments, but how does a less talented — but still good — junior player get onto the computer? Well, an amateur must play in a certain number of professional tournaments to get her ranking. But, how does she get into these tournaments?

Well, this player can start at satellites, where there isn't as much competition, and work her way up. Most tournaments, especially at the higher levels, hold qualifying rounds before the actual tournament begins. These qualifying rounds are like a mini-tournament in themselves. If the real tournament has four spots open for qualifiers, the top four players in the qualifying rounds — everyone who gets to the semifinals — is eligible to enter the main draw of the real tournament.

Sometimes, for a particularly big and prestigious tournament, so many people want to play, that the tournament has to hold *pre*qualifying rounds. In other words, players have to win the prequalifying rounds before they can even get into the qualifying rounds. Then, if the player wins the qualifying rounds, she can get into the main tournament. At that point, before the major tournament even begins, she has already played a lot of tennis matches.

If that isn't complicated enough, some players

are invited to play the qualifying rounds as "local" qualifiers. This is because they live within fifty miles of the actual tournament site. Other players may be invited to play the qualifying rounds based on past match performance, or because they have friends in the right places, at the right times. Still other players might just show up and hope for the best.

There is also a thing called a "wild card." If a player gets wild-carded into a tournament, that means she goes straight into the main draw, and gets to skip the qualifying rounds. Wild cards are hard to get — and every unranked player wants one. They are often given for reasons that seem based on favoritism. If a young player seems to have remarkable potential, an agent wooing her might make a few phone calls, and see if she or he can get the player into the tournament. Or, the group sponsoring the tournament may decide that a particular player would excite fans — because she is so young or has some other human-interest story to her — and so, the tournament will give the player a wild card. Many promising juniors get their first taste of professional tennis this way.

So, for a junior player more on the fringe than Jennifer was, achieving success on the professional tour can be frustrating, and difficult. But, when you get right down to it, a player who really is good enough to be a pro is going to get there even if she does run into a few roadblocks along the way.

Unlike sports where final results are decided upon by judges who could possibly be biased, or simply make a mistake, tennis is pretty black and white. Either you win your match, or you lose. Sometimes, a player might lose for reasons beyond her control, but on the whole, a player who is going to make it on the pro tour is able to rise above these things. Anyone who is going to be a champion expects some adversity, and knows how to handle it when it comes.

Some people might look at Jennifer, and decide that she has just been lucky, but Jennifer has earned the position she is in, every step of the way. She has met every challenge set before her — and met it easily.

And the next challenge was the French Open.

Chapter Seven

The French Open would be a big test for Jennifer because it was her first Grand Slam tournament, and she would have every reason to be very nervous. Of course, nobody told Jennifer that.

From the moment Jennifer hit Paris, and Roland Garros Stadium where the French Open is held, headlines like "Capriati Makes History" began to appear. Simply by winning her first match, she set another record: Jennifer became the youngest player *ever* to win a match in a Grand Slam tournament.

The French Open is played on clay courts — which suit steady baseline games — and is considered reflective of Paris itself. The atmosphere is a little calmer than it is at some of the other Grand Slams — namely, the U.S. Open — and almost elegant. Although serve-and-volleyers often run into trouble on the slow red clay surface, many players enjoy the continental feel of the tournament. Although Jennifer is not a traditional baseliner, she had spent so much time playing on clay courts in Florida, much as Chris Evert had before her, that the surface did not require much adjustment on her part. Also, Jennifer had played — and won — the Junior French Open the year before, so the setting was not completely unfamiliar.

Her first round was against Sandrine Testud, a French player who had been wild carded into the tournament as a local entry. The grandstands were crowded with fans, and even more reporters than usual. Jennifer won easily, 6–1, 6–1, and the throngs of fans were captivated.

Jennifer cruised through the early rounds of the tournament. Not even the fact that her third round match was scheduled for Center Court threw her off-balance. The Grand Slam tournaments are all held at large complexes, where matches are assigned to courts on the basis of anticipated fan interest. The most important matches, and the most important players, are always put on Center Court (Centre Court at Wimbledon, and Stadium Court at the U.S. Open), where the most seats are available for fans. Other prestigious matches are played in a slightly smaller nearby court, usually called Court 1, or the Grandstand Court. Lower-ranked players who lose in the early rounds rarely get anywhere near these two courts. In general, the higher the number of the court, the less important the tournament officials feel that particular match is.

Playing on one of the top two courts can be both an advantage and a disadvantage. Often, the condition of the court, and the quality of the lighting for night matches, is superior to the other courts. But, some players, faced with such a large audience — 15,000 to 30,000, depending on the size of the stadium — get so nervous that they are unable to play well. Other players thrive on the fan attention, and play even better than usual.

Jennifer, during her maiden Center Court match, thrived. She was facing an Austrian player, who was ranked number thirteen in the world, named Judith Wiesner. Jennifer lost the first two games — maybe just a tiny bit jittery — but then settled down and beat Judith in two sets, 6–4, 6–4.

Now, it was on to the round of sixteen — the quarterfinals — and with each victory, Jennifer continued her record-breaking performance, in this first Grand Slam tournament. It is worth mentioning that Jennifer was now ranked number 17 in the world on the WTA computer. Jennifer was to play Mercedes Paz, who had beaten the previous year's French Open champion, Arantxa Sanchez Vicario, to advance to the round of sixteen. Mercedes is from Argentina.

Jennifer took control right away, rolling through the first set, 6–0. Mercedes tried to rally in the second set, but Jennifer won the second set without much trouble, 6–3. This made Jennifer the youngest quarterfinalist in Grand Slam history — yet another record.

In the quarterfinals, Jennifer would have to play Mary Jo Fernandez, who was seeded seventh in the tournament. It would be a tough match.

Jennifer was not fazed at all. She beat Mary Jo, 6–2, 6–4 and, just like that, became the youngest semifinalist in Grand Slam history. The match had been held on Center Court again, but this time, Jennifer wasn't nervous at all.

Her semifinal match was against Monica Seles, who is from Yugoslavia, and all of sixteen years old. Monica, quite famous for her habit of grunting with every shot she makes, had won her last thirty matches in a row. Monica is also notable because not only does she have a two-handed backhand, but she also has a two-handed *forehand*. She would be a formidable opponent.

In fact, Monica was *too* formidable. Jennifer played hard, but Monica was in control all the way, with a relentless ground-stroke attack. Jennifer made too many unforced errors, and lost 6–2, 6–2, only holding her serve once. But, as Monica went on to win the entire tournament by defeating Steffi Graf, losing was certainly no disgrace. Jennifer didn't lose easily either, fighting off five consecutive match points before finally hitting a forehand long, to end the match. Jennifer and Monica are likely to have a long and exciting rivalry, and tennis fans can only hope it resembles the rivalry Chris Evert and Martina Navratilova had for so many years. There was no reason for Jennifer to be terribly disappointed by this first loss. She had played a superb tournament — and had had a good time in Paris too, getting in more than her fair share of sightseeing.

"I learned a lot," Jennifer said, "getting to the semi's. Monica and I are both pretty young, and I hope we're around for a long time."

And now, Jennifer was ranked thirteenth in the world. Wimbledon — the biggest tournament in all of tennis — would be next.

Chapter Eight

All of the Grand Slam tournaments are important, but it would be hard to find a tennis player — professional *or* amateur — who wouldn't rather win Wimbledon than any other tournament in the world. It is a tournament steeped with tradition — and with royalty. The Royal Family has a Royal Box at Centre Court, and often the Queen, or Princess Di, will be sitting there, watching the tennis. Many members of the Royal Family show up throughout the tournament, especially for the finals, and later congratulate the winners in person.

Wimbledon is played on grass, which is the most challenging of all tennis surfaces. This is fitting, since Wimbledon is the most challenging tournament of all. Grass is a tough surface because it is very fast, and it is often uneven. Despite the best groundskeeping imaginable, the grass gets worn away — especially near the service lines — and tiny divots of grass get kicked up as players run and skid towards balls. It is hard to adjust to grass, especially right after playing on the slow clay surface of the French Open. Balls bounce and skip unpredictably on grass, and the surface definitely favors serve-and-volleyers. As the grass wears away during the tournament, a good server's serves get even faster and more unhittable than usual.

Jennifer's first match was on Centre Court, against Helen Kelesi of Canada. Jennifer won easily, 6–3, 6–1. Once again, Jennifer was beyond "nerves." And yes, this made her the youngest player ever to win at a match at Wimbledon. No matter what Jennifer did, she seemed to break a record doing it.

She coasted right into the round of sixteen — and right into Steffi Graf. Steffi was the only one of the top players in the world who Jennifer had yet to face in her brief career, and Steffi was the number *one* player in the world.

Centre Court was jammed with spectators, including the Duchess of York — perhaps better known as "Fergie." Steffi, all of twenty-one years old, was the cagy veteran in this pair. She was also too good for Jennifer, winning 6–2, 6–4, the match lasting less than an hour. But, Jennifer was happy to have gotten as far as the quarterfinals.

"Playing Steffi on Centre Court — that was

great," Jennifer said later. "It was a great experience."

In Jennifer's first six pro tournaments, she had ended up facing the four best players in the world — Martina, Gabriela, Monica, and Steffi. (After her tremendous performance at Wimbledon, Zina Garrison moved into this group, with a top-five ranking.) Jennifer hadn't been able to beat any of them — hadn't even really come close — but, none of the defeats had been lopsided.

"I'm definitely not top-five," Jennifer said later, "I've played them, but I haven't really come close to beating them. I'm going to have to develop a better serve, and just be more aggressive."

This fourteen-year-old might not yet be one of the top five players in the world, but, clearly, she is knocking on the door.

The United States Tennis Association must have agreed with this assessment because, after Wimbledon, Jennifer was named to the United States Federation Cup Team. (The women's Federation Cup is equivalent to the men's Davis Cup competition.) Being selected to play on this team is considered a great honor. In the Federation Cup, countries from all over the world send teams to compete against one another. It is sort of like a professional Olympics.

Zina Garrison, Mary Joe Fernandez, and Gigi Fernandez (Mary Joe and Gigi are not related) were named to the team, along with Jennifer. The Cup competition was to be held in July in Norcross, Georgia, which is near Atlanta. The United States team was hoping to win, and defend their championship from 1989.

Some of the other countries that were competing included France, Great Britain, Mexico, West Germany, and the USSR. Teams came from as far away as Trinidad and Tobago, Taipei, and Malaysia.

In the first round, the United States was slated to play the team from Poland. There would be three matches — two singles and one doubles match — and the winning country would advance to the next round. Jennifer beat Magdalena Mroz, while Zina defeated Katarzyna Nowak. Then, Zina and Gigi won their doubles match, to give the United States a convincing 3–0 victory over the Polish team.

The United States moved on to the quarterfinals by beating Belgium — again, 3–0. Jennifer beat Sandra Wasserman in singles, while Zina was taking her singles match from Sabine Applemans. Then, Zina and Gigi beat Sandra and Sabine in doubles.

Next, Jennifer and her teammates would meet the Czechoslovakian team. They won, 2–1, and it was on to the semifinals, where they defeated Austria by a score of 3–0.

Now, the United States only had to win one more match to retain their championship crown. Their opponent was the team from the Soviet Union. The USSR put up a good fight, but Jennifer

51

and her teammates emerged victorious, with a 2–1 win. Once again, the United States had won the Federation Cup. Jennifer and her teammates were very proud.

It had been a long few months of tennis, and now it was time for Jennifer to go home to Florida and take a much-deserved vacation. But, she was still bubbling over with enthusiasm about her first trip to Europe as a professional.

"I thought it was wonderful," she said. "I thought Wimbledon was especially cool."

Going home and seeing her friends would be cool, too.

Chapter Nine

What is day-to-day life like for a professional tennis player? In many ways it is glamourous, but it can also be very difficult, and exhausting.

Professional tennis players travel and travel, and then travel some more. Most players play at least twenty tournaments a year, which is almost two a month. A tournament is a week long, if a player keeps winning, and since most pros play both singles and doubles, they usually have to stay around for one competition, even if they've already lost in the other category.

There are tournaments all over the world, and with all that travel time, a player doesn't get much time at home — or very many days off. A tennis player spends more time on planes, waiting in airports, and sitting in unfamiliar hotel rooms than she does actually playing tennis. Crossing time zones and eating strange food and drinking strange water can really do a number on a player's health and energy.

Jennifer's parents are smart to encourage Jennifer to behave like a tourist in the exciting cities she visits, as well as like a professional tennis player. Surprisingly, this is not a common practice. There are players who have been going to Wimbledon for years and yet, have never really explored London. Not only is sightseeing interesting, but it is also educational. It is too easy for a tennis player to get so engrossed in her tennis that she shuts out everything else. It is important, of course, for a player to be able to concentrate fully on tennis during a tournament, but an athletic career doesn't last forever, and it is a good idea for a player to remember that there is a whole big world out there that *doesn't* revolve around tennis.

The prize money on the tennis tour is high, but expenses are high, too. Right now, it is safe to estimate that a year's expenses on the tour will come to about fifty thousand dollars. Airfare will probably be a good twenty thousand dollars worth of this, with another ten thousand to cover hotel bills. Then, a player has to add in the cost of food, medical bills, telephone calls, equipment not provided by endorsement contracts, and personal items. An agent or management firm will take anywhere between ten and twenty-five percent of a player's prize money and endorsement fees.

Jennifer usually travels with at least one of her parents, and often her entire family. Her agent, John Evert, is generally along for the trip, plus her coach, Tom Gullickson, and her hitting partner, Richard Ashby. The tour can be very lonely, especially for a young player, and it is important that she have at least one traveling companion.

The most important person a player can bring along is a coach. A traveling coach is expensive, but invaluable. A coach is also a luxury not all players can afford. A coach not only helps with tactics and match strategy, but also can be a dinner partner, a friend, and sometimes even a surrogate parent. A coach has to keep his or her player happy, healthy, and confident. A coach congratulates a player when she wins, and cheers her up when she loses. A pro coach is always there to listen and advise and encourage. In many ways, helping a player with her game may be the least of a coach's duties. Helping a player find a way to do her laundry on the road, or making sure she eats a good breakfast and gets enough sleep, is often more important. And again, it is even more important when the player is young.

A player like Jennifer, who is still in school, has the added complication of homework. Jennifer takes courses by correspondence, her teachers mailing or faxing her assignments, which she then completes, and sends back. An older player doesn't have to worry about going up to her room to do her algebra right after winning her quarterfinal match.

"I've learned a lot in all the European places," Jennifer says. "Just sightseeing, you learn a lot."

Many young players from countries other than the United States never even complete high school, putting their careers first. This may work in the short run, but even the greatest of tennis players rarely play beyond their mid-thirties. Even if the retiring player is financially set for life, thirty-five — if she even plays that long — is mighty young to spend the rest of your life lounging around. A player needs to plan ahead, and if she doesn't even have a high school education, she isn't going to have very many career options. Some players go into coaching and broadcasting — but there are only so many spots open in those fields. On top of which, broadcasting requires a person who is articulate and very knowledgeable — about more than just tennis. A player without any education isn't likely to fall into that category. Players often say that they will go back to school when their careers are over, but very few do. The greatest role model of all might be a player who has a brilliant tennis career, and then goes on to have another brilliant career in a field like education or law or medicine. Thirty-five may seem old to a young player just starting out, but quitting school is nothing if not shortsighted. Even the best player in the world can suffer a career-ending injury, and it is important to have other options in life.

So, Jennifer is continuing her education while she is on the road, and she attends regular classes when she is at home. This is probably one of the biggest reasons that she is so refreshingly normal, and able to approach her career with a certain amount of perspective. Her parents will help her keep this attitude, and over the long haul, it will help her tennis — and help her be a happy and fulfilled person after she retires.

And how does Jennifer feel about the tour after spending a little time on it? Does she get along with the other players?

"I think on the tour, there's not many kids my age playing," Jennifer said recently. "At first, it took them [the other players] a little while, but they're all nice to me. Monica is a little more my age, but they're all pretty cool. Even though I'm around adults, I'm still having fun. When I come home, that's when I see my friends who are my age."

And how do her friends at home feel about all of Jennifer's success?

"They're interested in what went on," Jennifer said, "and they're proud of me, and they congratulate me, but they don't treat me any different. I still lead a normal life."

Leading a normal life may well be the secret to all of Jennifer's success.

So, what happens when a player actually gets to a professional tournament? Most tournaments have a "tournament" hotel locally that offers reduced rates to players. Generally, a player will check into this hotel. A small tournament may not have a designated hotel, but will provide host families for a player to stay with instead. This is great if the player and her host family hit it off, but it can be very stressful if they don't. Even if the player and the host family do like one another, staying at a perfect stranger's house can be a little bit hard.

After signing in at the actual tournament location, and checking the draw for her first round opponent and the time of her first match, a player has to arrange for a time to practice, and a place to practice. At some tournaments — especially indoor tournaments — practice courts are at a premium, and a player will often have to practice *with* her opponents. This can help friendships form, but it doesn't always accomplish much along the lines of serious match preparation. At the Virginia Slims Championships, for example, there is only one practice court, because the tournament is held inside Madison Square Garden, in New York City. A player can either try to find a period of time when the court is free, or she can try to make arrangements to find some other place to practice. In New York City, a tennis court can be pretty hard to find.

Most tournaments provide buses, or cars driven by volunteers, to help players get from place to place. The bigger tournaments, logically enough, provide more services than smaller tournaments. There will usually be a doctor or two to examine complaints of illness or injury, and there is often a masseuse, too. The players' lounge is set up with food and drinks, and telephones are provided for the players' convenience. If a player needs practice balls, or aspirin, or recommendations for local restaurants, tournament officials will be there to provide whatever is needed.

Then, there is the press. A player of Jennifer's caliber will usually have to hold a press conference when she arrives at the tournament, hold another press conference after each match, and then hold a final conference at the end of her last match. There are always writers and television reporters around, most of whom are eager to get a few minutes alone with players for exclusive interviews, and it is hard for someone like Jennifer to get any time to herself at all. Jennifer's family and entourage do their best to keep her insulated from all of this attention, but this can be almost impossible when a microphone appears every time Jennifer opens her mouth, and a camera bulb flashes every time she moves. So far, Jennifer has received more media attention than almost any new player in memory. The more she wins, the more attention she will receive. Answering the same questions over and over is part of a player's job, but it can get very tiring. If Jennifer wants to go out somewhere, even to a local mall, a television crew and reporters will often come along. Life is no longer as spontaneous as it once was, and it can be tough to adjust to this. One of the most impressive things about Jennifer is the way she has handled all of this overwhelming attention.

"I've learned to block it out," Jennifer says. "I just ignore it when it gets to be a little much. I'm having fun."

Then, there are the fans. Many tournaments are informal enough for fans to be able to go right up to players to request autographs or pictures and ask questions. This can be fun, but it is also hard work.

A player also has responsibilities relating to her endorsements. She may have to take time away from the tournament to meet and greet employees and investors from her racket company, to pose for print ads, or even to shoot a commercial. If, for example, Prince holds a publicity party for its newest racket or fashion products in the city where Jennifer is playing a tournament, she would probably be expected to attend the party as a representative. This is part of the business of being a professional tennis player, but a person only has so much energy, and having too many outside responsibilities can make it difficult to concentrate on the player's *real* job — playing tennis. This is why Jennifer's parents and agent are so careful to limit Jennifer's endorsements and professional responsibilities.

All in all, being a professional tennis player can be fun and rewarding, but it isn't easy. A lot more work is involved than just swinging a racket a few times a day. Sometimes, playing tennis is the easy part.

Chapter Ten

Jennifer's next tournament was the Mt. Cranmore International Women's Tennis Championships, held in North Conway, New Hampshire. This was a fairly small tournament, and Jennifer would be the highest-ranking player in attendance. The second seed was Laura Gildemeister, who Jennifer had beaten back at her debut tournament in Boca Raton.

This was the first time this particular tournament had been held, and the tournament directors were very happy that Jennifer would be making her first New England appearance at Mt. Cranmore. North Conway is very popular with tourists in the summer, and a good turnout of fans was expected. For her part, Jennifer was probably happy to be playing at a tournament with a slightly lower profile than usual. Also, the tournament was being played on clay courts, a surface Jennifer enjoyed. If Jennifer could win at Mt. Cranmore, it would be her first professional championship.

"If I win this, it'll be a good memory," Jennifer admitted at a press conference early in the tournament.

Jennifer was also happy to be in New Hampshire, a place where she had never been before. North Conway is located right in the heart of ski country, surrounded by mountains.

"North Conway is beautiful," she said. "I'm really fascinated by the mountains, because in Florida there aren't any mountains. It's pretty cool."

Because Jennifer was so highly ranked, and had been playing in the Federation Cup right before the beginning of the Mt. Cranmore tournament, the tournament officials decided that Jennifer should skip the first two rounds of the tournament, and play her first match in the quarterfinals. When a player skips a round, it is called "being given a bye." Small tournaments like to have the best players come and, realizing how little time a pro has, they often give her a "bye" or two, so she will have to spend fewer days at the tournament and so will be more likely to be able to attend. Although lower-ranked players often resent this practice, it is a privilege that the top players have earned — and byes are not uncommon for them.

Jennifer's quarterfinal opponent was nineteen-year-old Stacey Martin. Stacey is the same sort of hard-hitting, hustling player that Jennifer is, but — at this point, anyway — she is not close to being in Jennifer's league. Jennifer made a lot of unforced errors, had problems with her serve — and still won without much trouble, 6–4, 7–5. Jennifer played unevenly — winning several games in a row, then losing a few, then winning a few more in a row.

"I made a lot of double faults," Jennifer said after the match. "I guess it was a day when it wasn't going right. She played really well. I thought the main thing was to get my first serve in, and just play tough."

With that victory, Jennifer was in the semifinals, against Susan Sloane. The only real mistake Jennifer made was to lose track of the score at one point and sit down for the changeover before the game was actually over. After recovering from that momentary embarrassment, Jennifer went on to win, 6–2, 6–2. Her game was much steadier than it had been the day before, and Jennifer would be going into the finals with plenty of confidence.

The other finalist was Ros Fairbank, who was born in South Africa, and now lives in the United States. Ros was ranked number 25 in the world, while Jennifer was still ranked number 13.

It was very sunny and hot, and Jennifer got a good start by winning the first set, 6–3. But, Ros came back to take the second set, also by a score of 6–3. Jennifer had to bear down in the third set, and suddenly, she was serving for the match. If she could win this game, she would have her first championship as a professional.

When she won the last point, it was a very big moment. She had won twenty-five thousand dollars, but — more importantly — she had set another milestone in her career. She was the champion of the Mt. Cranmore International Women's Tennis Championships. With luck, it would only be the first in a long series of championships for Jennifer.

The U.S. Open was looming ahead, but Jennifer went to the Player's Challenge in Montreal first. A lot of other top players were there, getting ready for the Open, so the competition was very strong.

Jennifer made her way easily through the first three rounds, gaining two-set wins over players like Lisa Green and Camille Benjamin, both of whom are Americans. She was playing well, but in the quarterfinals, she was scheduled to play Gabriela Sabatini again. And, unfortunately, Jennifer lost again.

This time, though, the match was closer, Jennifer pushing it to the full three sets. The final score was 3–6, 6–1, 6–4. Next time she played Gabriela, maybe she would win.

Jennifer played one more tune-up tournament before the Open, a small exhibition tournament called the Pathmark Classic. It was held in Mahwah, New Jersey, not far from New York City.

Jennifer made it all the way to the finals, where she faced Steffi Graf again. She didn't win — but like her match with Gabriela in Montreal — she played well enough to push the match to three sets before Steffi prevailed. Steffi does not lose very many sets, so Jennifer was encouraged by this result.

Jennifer still wasn't there, but her knocks on the door leading to the top five were getting louder.

Chapter Eleven

When people start talking about young tennis players, people generally start talking about burnout. Burnout is one of the biggest problems in tennis today, and yet, also one of the most misunderstood. Young athletes with apparently unlimited potential come, and they go, and the sad truth is, mostly they go. Why does this happen, and can it be prevented?

As discussed in earlier chapters, the life of a professional tennis player can be grueling. When a player is very young, the normal stresses and strains can be even more difficult to handle. A player who is successful has to face the pressures of fan expectations and the spotlight of the media. The hard thing about tennis is that once you win, you have to keep winning to maintain your ranking and status. A player who doesn't win has even more problems. There is the problem of making enough money to make ends meet, there is the problem of getting into tournaments without playing qualifying rounds, there is the problem of coping with perceived failure.

One of the most difficult things for a player to accept is the way she is perceived by others. Even avid tennis fans can rarely name many players below the top twenty or so, and many probably can't even name that many. Everyone has heard of the same five or ten players, and that's about it. The attitude that only being the best is good enough often prevails. This is very unfortunate. In almost every other profession, a person who was considered among the top fifty, or one hundred, or two hundred, in the world, would feel like a tremendous success. After all, the world is a pretty big place. Not everyone can be number one, and just being a professional tennis player — regardless of your ranking — is pretty impressive in itself.

The fact that Jennifer, a fourteen-year-old, has done as well as she has, should be enough. But, instead of just applauding what she has already accomplished, there is a tendency to ask, "What next?" People wonder when she is going to win a Grand Slam, when she is going to beat Steffi, if she will become number one. There would probably be a lot less burnout among players if the prevailing attitude were, "Good for you, good luck!" It would make more sense to let a player proceed at her own pace, rather than adding more pressure to achieve. Jennifer seems to be the rare type of player, and person, who can rise above these pressures, but it's too bad that they exist at all.

What exactly is burnout anyway? It is hard to define, but there are two basic types: mental and physical. The perception is that mental burnout is sort of like cracking up under all that pressure, and that a player quits because she can no longer cope. In some cases, this may be true, but not in most cases. Players who are unable to handle all of the pressure would be apt to stop playing at the junior level well before they turn pro.

It is often assumed, if a player takes a vacation, that she is burned-out. On the other hand, there is nothing abnormal about taking a vacation, and maybe the player just wants to take some time off and relax. This should probably be encouraged, rather than criticized.

Is it also burnout when a player just plain decides to stop playing, and move on to something else? Consider that the average player has been playing tennis since she was a toddler, and tennis has been the focus of her life ever since. As a person grows older, she or he has a tendency to develop other interests. Maybe the player wants the chance to lead a less hectic life; maybe the player has just come across something she finds more interesting. Phrases other than burnout could be used to describe this, like "broadening your horizons" and "changing your mind." Many people change careers, and there is no reason why tennis players shouldn't do so, too. It is too easy to pin the stigma of burnout onto the players. True mental burnout happens now and again, but it certainly would be the exception, rather than the rule.

A player can also physically burn-out, and this type of burnout is probably more common. Tennis is a demanding sport, and a player's body takes a lot of pounding and abuse. The tour goes on pretty much throughout the year, and the playing surfaces change constantly. Injuries are an unfortunate, but unavoidable consequence. When a football player, for example, suffers a severe knee injury, nobody says he burned-out; they just say that he got hurt. It is the same in tennis. Players get hurt. Sometimes, they can continue playing; sometimes, they can't. Baseball pitcher and Hall-of-Famer Sandy Koufax quit at the peak of his career because he didn't want to put his arm through all that pain anymore, or cause any further damage. It takes a mature athlete to make a decision like that.

Often, the question of physical burnout in women's tennis comes up because the players are so young. However, as long as the player's parents keep a close eye on their child, and make sure she gets regular, specialized medical checkups, and is put on a careful and well-planned conditioning program, there is no reason why she shouldn't

play. An unforseen injury can always happen —
but people also slip on ice, or fall down the stairs,
and get hurt. No one would ever call *that* burnout.

Jennifer's parents and coaches have been very
cautious when it comes to Jennifer's physical well-
being. They have taken her, more than once, to
the Virginia Sportsmedicine Institute for physical
and psychological tests. Jennifer tested as high as
a person can test, mainly because she has not for-
gotten that tennis is supposed to be a game, and
that she is supposed to be having fun.

"When you don't have fun, that's when you get
frustrated," she has said since.

Medical science has advanced to the degree that
the level of testing is extremely sophisticated.
Everything from the way a player moves and hits
the ball to her muscle density to her percentage
of body fat is calculated. During Jennifer's first
visit, the doctors did find a weakness in her right
shoulder — possibly caused by the constant mo-
tion of serving. She was immediately put on a special conditioning program to correct this problem,
and now her shoulder is stronger than ever. The
reason checkups are so important for players is
that doctors can find a problem before it really *is*
a problem. In fact, after following the new conditioning program, Jennifer's progress in all areas
was significant. For example, she went from being
able to do 42 sit-ups in one minute, to being able
to do 61. Her grip strength changed from 72
pounds to 86 pounds. She went from 16 push-ups

a minute to 35. As long as Jennifer's physical fitness is regularly monitored, and her parents continue to keep her from overdoing it, physical burnout should not be a problem.

The two players who are always used as ultimate examples of burnout are Tracy Austin and Andrea Jaeger. But, a closer look at both cases may contradict this assessment.

When Tracy Austin came onto the scene as a young teenager, she won everything in sight. She was a quarterfinalist at the U.S. Open in 1977, and then *won* the U.S Open in 1979, when she was only sixteen years old. She won tournament after tournament, and everyone was sure she would take over the crown as the Queen of Tennis from Chris Evert. She and Chris and Martina had all been trading places at number one, as the top three players in the world. Tracy's potential seemed to know no bounds. She was a classic baseliner, her style very much like Chris Evert's. And yet, by 1983, Tracy Austin was almost completely out of tennis, barely twenty years old, and suffering from a number of injuries. The verdict was: burnout.

Tracy had shoulder and foot injuries, but the most serious problem was her chronically bad back. She had a number of back ailments, but sciatica was the most serious problem. Some people feel that her back troubles began because she had spent so many hours on hard tennis courts, when her body wasn't mature enough to take the stresses of this. Other people feel that the injuries were just bad luck. Tracy's back never really recovered, but she tried to make several comebacks. Because she was overcompensating for her back, she developed other injuries, and finally had to make the decision to retire. This was very unfortunate — but it probably *wasn't* burnout, any more than Joe Namath's decision to retire because of his bad knees was burnout.

Andrea Jaeger ran into the same sort of unhappy situation early in her career. She turned pro in 1980, when she was fourteen years old. By the time she was nineteen, she was no longer playing professional tennis. She won her first pro tournament at thirteen as an amateur, and was once ranked number two in the world. Like Tracy, Andrea beat everyone in sight. Most people assumed that the pressure had gotten to her, and that's why she quit.

Andrea was a player in the Billie Jean King mold — small and feisty and tough. She suffered a number of injuries, and made the mistake of trying to "play through" them. Too many coaches encourage this attitude, rather than teaching their players to take time off to heal. This is especially important with young players, who are sometimes too eager to play, and need someone to tell them to take it easy, that there is always another day and another match.

Andrea's most serious injury was to her serving shoulder, and although she has had extraordinary corrective surgery, she has never recovered enough to be able to take the physical stresses of the tour again. She had many other injuries, including one that was diagnosed as a strained muscle, and turned out to be a broken pelvis. Perhaps if her injuries had been diagnosed earlier, most of her physical problems could have been treated and minimized, and she might still be on the tour today. After retiring, Andrea has used her time well, and went to college to further her education.

Despite the bad luck these two players suffered, other young juniors continue to turn pro in record numbers. And, as coaches and doctors learn more about sports medicine, they are better able to watch and protect these young players from unnecessary physical strain.

In just about every interview, Jennifer is asked if she, too, expects to suffer some form of burnout. She handles this question politely, but obviously gets tired of it.

"I'm kind of like, why do they keep asking me these questions," she said in a recent interview. "I'm sort of tired of it. I get good supervision. I go to the gym and do exercises for specific muscles. Just because it happened to some people, doesn't mean it will happen to everyone. I *don't* think it's going to happen to me."

Reporters also, inevitably, ask Jennifer how much stress she feels. This is a question Jennifer tosses off with a genuine shrug.

"I'm not really feeling that much pressure," she said, after a match at Mt. Cranmore. "I'm just going out there and having fun. I'm just thinking it's kind of neat. It's some excitement for me."

With Jennifer's personality, and that attitude, she is not likely to suffer from burnout. She may, at some point, decide that she wants to do something else with her life, but that's up to her. Until that day, with luck, reporters will just sit back along with everyone else, and enjoy the show.

Chapter Twelve

The U.S. Open is held in New York City, and it is big and loud and full of energy. Some players hate it more than any other tournament; other players get more excited about playing in New York than anyplace else. Jennifer in in the latter group. She was born in New York, and Jennifer couldn't wait to play the U.S. Open.

"I'm really psyched," she said, shortly before the tournament began, "that I get to play in front of my home crowd."

The U.S. Open is held at Flushing Meadow, near Shea Stadium, where the Mets play. It has a stadium court, with room for over twenty thousand spectators, and a grandstand court, with room for just over six thousand fans. There are twenty-seven courts in all, and Court 16, with room for four thousand, is the next most prestigious place for a match to be assigned. The complex offers plenty of souvenirs and snacks — and all of them are expensive. In years past, the worst problem at Flushing Meadow has been the number of jets taking off from nearby La Guardia Airport, and flying directly over the stadium, drowning out all sounds. In 1990, New York City Mayor David Dinkins negotiated to have air traffic sent in a different direction during the Open, which made the atmosphere more relaxing. Mayor Dinkins, you see, plays a little tennis himself.

While Wimbledon — and even the French Open — has a very exclusive feel, the U.S. Open is brash and friendly, with a thoroughly American style. It is always noisy, and the stands are always jam-packed. For a player as cheerful and gregarious as Jennifer, it is a terrific place to be. From the moment she got to the grounds at Flushing Meadow, she was the most popular person around, unable to walk anywhere without being beseiged by autograph seekers. Almost all of the fans following her around were teenagers and children, and none of them went away disappointed.

Right as the tournament began, the Women's Tennis Association held their annual awards dinner. A number of prizes were given, and the dinner raised a quarter of a million dollars for the March of Dimes.

Jennifer won the award for Most Impressive Newcomer and, during her acceptance speech, referred to Mayor Dinkins as "a cool dude." (Monica Seles was also memorable, referring to the mayor as "Major" Dinkins.) Other award winners included Steffi Graf, as Player of the Year, Monica Seles, as Most Improved Player, and Mercedes Paz, who was given the Karen Krantzcke Sportsmanship Award.

But now, it was time to play tennis.

Wearing her peace earrings, Jennifer was ready to go. Her first round was against Anke Huber, a fifteen-year-old from West Germany. It was a night match, and it was being held on the stadium court. Jennifer was a little nervous, but she came out fast, winning the first four games of the set. Anke turned right around and took the next five games in a row, for a 5–4 lead. Then, Jennifer turned it around again, and won the next three games, to win the set.

Jennifer and Anke both have very powerful ground strokes, and they spent most of the match whacking the ball at each other as hard as they could. Play was fast and furious, and fun to watch.

The second set went pretty much the same way. Jennifer came out hard, faltered a little, then finished strong. Anke is a good player, who a number of people are pegging as the "next" Steffi Graf, but Jennifer prevailed, with a 7–5, 7–5 victory.

Jennifer had a lot of fun at the U.S. Open, and perhaps the highlight of her tournament was the night she was watching John McEnroe play on the stadium court. John is also a native New Yorker, making a fine effort on the comeback trail. Jennifer was sitting in a box of seats with Wilt Chamberlain — which was fun. But then, it got *really* fun. Tom Cruise showed up. For Jennifer, sitting and watching tennis with Tom Cruise was about as good as it gets.

Jennifer moved easily through the early rounds of the tournament — on a direct collision course with Steffi Graf. They met in the round of sixteen. The stadium was packed. Jennifer had been encouraged by her good performance against Steffi at the Pathmark Classics in New Jersey, but she was also more nervous than usual. The crowd was solidly behind Jennifer, but she was overhitting, and many of her shots went out-of-bounds. To make matters worse, Steffi played like a woman on a mission. With style and experience and power, Steffi made it look easy, winning the match in less than an hour. Jennifer put up a good effort, especially in the early part of the second set, but Steffi was just too good. The final score was 6–1, 6–2.

Despite that loss — to the number one player in the world, after all — Jennifer had every reason to be happy. Her record as a professional player was forty-three victories, against only nine defeats. That is an excellent record for any player — and absolutely extraordinary for a fourteen-year-old. Jennifer had more than lived up to anyone's expectations — maybe even her own.

There was more good news after the U.S. Open

ended, with Gabriela Sabatini the eventual winner over Steffi Graf. The new WTA computer rankings came out.

After only six months as a professional tennis player, Jennifer was now ranked number 12 in the world.

Chapter Thirteen

There have been many talented, young professional athletes. Some, like Jennifer, have experienced immediate and spectacular success. Others have never gotten beyond solid middle rankings. Some have stayed on the tour for years, while others have played for a while, then moved on to college, and other careers.

The future of women's tennis is very exciting, with young stars like Jennifer, Monica Seles, Mary Joe Fernandez, Arantxa Sanchez Vicario, and Gabriela Sabatini. Steffi Graf is only twenty-one. The 1990s promise to be a great decade for women's tennis.

There are many fine young male tennis professionals, too. Nineteen-year-old Pete Sampras won the 1990 U.S. Open title. Michael Chang won the French Open as a seventeen-year-old, and Andre Agassi has gotten to several Grand Slam finals as a teenager. Boris Becker, who won Wimbledon at seventeen, is only twenty-one now. There are many exciting rivalries ahead in both women's and men's tennis.

"I'm glad I'm doing this," Jennifer said, when asked how she felt about being on the tennis tour. "It's a great experience. The pro level is definitely higher than the juniors. The top players all have different kinds of games. I knew it was going to be tough, and I'm just happy I've gotten the chance to play."

Jennifer also feels a big responsibility towards her fans.

"I receive a lot of letters from kids my age," she said. "They say they really get inspired by me, and that's what I want. It gives me a lot of confidence, it helps me a lot."

When asked about her ambitions in the game, Jennifer smiled. "I've never thought about doing anything else," she said, referring to her tennis career. "I've known from the start that that's what I wanted to do. I hope to become the top one, but it's really going to take a lot. I'm just going to do the best I can. I'm having fun."

What comes next for Jennifer? Well, school,

mainly. Right after the U.S. Open, Jennifer went back to Florida, to attend the St. Andrews school. There would be a couple more tournaments in 1990, but for now, it was time to be fourteen again for a while.

Career Highlights

Capriati's Junior Career

1988

Omega Easter Bowl 16-and-under Champion
USTA National Hard Court Champion
USTA National Clay Court Champion
Selected 1988 "Junior Player of the Year" by *Tennis* magazine and *World Tennis* magazine.
Selected 1988 "Most Promising Junior Player of the Year" by *Seventeen* magazine.

1989

U.S. Open Junior Champion, Singles
U.S. Open Junior Champion, Doubles
Junior French Open Champion
Junior Wimbledon Champion, Doubles
Junior Wimbledon Quarterfinalist, Singles

Capriati's Professional Career

1990

Championships Champion, Mt. Cranmore International Women's Tennis

Virginia Slims of Florida, Singles Finalist. Youngest player ever to make her professional debut. Reached the finals of her first tournament.

Family Circle Magazine Cup, Singles Finalist.

French Open, Semifinalist. Youngest player ever to win a match at a Grand Slam tournament.

Wimbledon, Quarterfinalist. Youngest player ever to win a match at Wimbledon.

U.S. Open, Quarterfinalist

Selected to the Federation Cup Team, with Zina Garrison, Mary Joe Fernandez, and Gigi Fernandez. The United States won the Federation Cup, defeating the Soviet Union in the finals.

SCHOLASTIC BIOGRAPHY

❏ MP44075-6	Bo Jackson: Playing the Games	$2.95
❏ MP41836-X	Custer and Crazy Horse: A Story of Two Warriors	$2.75
❏ MP44570-7	The Death of Lincoln: A Picture History of the Assassination	$2.95
❏ MP43866-2	The Defenders	$2.75
❏ MP43210-9	Faithful Friend: The Story of Florence Nightingale	$2.75
❏ MP44767-X	The First Woman Doctor	$2.95
❏ MP42218-9	Frederick Douglass Fights for Freedom	$2.50
❏ MP43628-7	Freedom Train: The Story of Harriet Tubman	$2.75
❏ MP43730-5	George Washington: The Man Who Would Not Be King	$2.75
❏ MP43800-X	Great Escapes of World War II	$2.75
❏ MP42402-5	Harry Houdini: Master of Magic	$2.75
❏ MP42404-1	Helen Keller	$2.50
❏ MP44230-9	I Have a Dream: The Story of Martin Luther King	$2.50
❏ MP42395-9	Jesse Jackson: A Biography	$2.75
❏ MP43503-5	Jim Abbott: Against All Odds	$2.75
❏ MP41344-9	John Fitzgerald Kennedy: America's 35th President	$2.50
❏ MP41159-4	Lost Star: The Story of Amelia Earhart	$2.75
❏ MP42659-1	Mr. President: A Book of U.S. Presidents	$2.75
❏ MP42644-3	Our 41st President George Bush	$2.50
❏ MP43481-0	Pocahontas and the Strangers	$2.75
❏ MP41877-7	Ready, Aim, Fire! The Real Adventures of Annie Oakley	$2.75
❏ MP41183-7	Secret Missions: Four True-Life Stories	$2.50
❏ MP43052-1	The Secret Soldier: The Story of Deborah Sampson	$2.50
❏ MP43605-8	Sole Survivor	$2.95
❏ MP44055-1	Squanto, Friend of the Pilgrims	$2.75
❏ MP42560-9	Stealing Home: The Story of Jackie Robinson	$2.75
❏ MP44353-4	The Story of My Life	$2.75
❏ MP42403-3	The Story of Thomas Alva Edison, Inventor: The Wizard of Menlo Park	$2.50
❏ MP44431-X	They Led the Way: 14 American Women	$2.95
❏ MP42904-3	The Wright Brothers at Kitty Hawk	$2.75

Available wherever you buy books, or use this order form.

Scholastic Inc., P.O. Box 7502, 2931 East McCarty Street, Jefferson City, MO 65102

Please send me the books I have checked above. I am enclosing $_____ (please add $2.00 to cover shipping and handling). Send check or money order — no cash or C.O.D.s please.

Name_____

Address_____

City_____ State/Zip _____

Please allow four to six weeks for delivery. Available in the U.S. only. Sorry, mail orders are not available to residents of Canada. Prices subject to change.

BIO1190

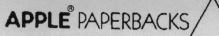

APPLE® PAPERBACKS

Pick an Apple and Polish Off Some Great Reading!

BEST-SELLING APPLE TITLES

☐ MT42975-2	**The Bullies and Me** Harriet Savitz	$2.75
☐ MT42709-1	**Christina's Ghost** Betty Ren Wright	$2.75
☐ MT41682-0	**Dear Dad, Love Laurie** Susan Beth Pfeffer	$2.75
☐ MT43461-6	**The Dollhouse Murders** Betty Ren Wright	$2.75
☐ MT42545-5	**Four Month Friend** Susan Clymer	$2.75
☐ MT43444-6	**Ghosts Beneath Our Feet** . Betty Ren Wright	$2.75
☐ MT44351-8	**Help! I'm a Prisoner in the Library** Eth Clifford	$2.75
☐ MT43188-9	**The Latchkey Kids** Carol Anshaw	$2.75
☐ MT44567-7	**Leah's Song** Eth Clifford	$2.75
☐ MT43618-X	**Me and Katie (The Pest)** Ann M. Martin	$2.75
☐ MT41529-8	**My Sister, The Creep** Candice F. Ransom	$2.75
☐ MT42883-7	**Sixth Grade Can Really Kill You** Barthe DeClements	$2.75
☐ MT40409-1	**Sixth Grade Secrets** Louis Sachar	$2.75
☐ MT42882-9	**Sixth Grade Sleepover** Eve Bunting	$2.75
☐ MT41732-0	**Too Many Murphys** Colleen O'Shaughnessy McKenna	$2.75
☐ MT42326-6	**Veronica the Show-Off** Nancy K. Robinson	$2.75

Available wherever you buy books, or use this order form.

Scholastic Inc., P.O. Box 7502, 2931 East McCarty Street, Jefferson City, MO 65102

Please send me the books I have checked above. I am enclosing $_____ (please add $2.00 to cover shipping and handling). Send check or money order — no cash or C.O.D.s please.

Name _____

Address _____

City_____ State/Zip _____

Please allow four to six weeks for delivery. Offer good in the U.S.A. only. Sorry, mail orders are not available to residents of Canada. Prices subject to change.

APP1090

PB

PB   C.1

White, Ellen Emerson
    Jennifer Capriati